Angelica -

Perhaps on [illegible] ill
take a trip t[illegible]
wonderful elephants in person -
until then, I hope you enjoy
the pictures in this book.

Love -
Grandma
Christmas, 2012

An Elephant's Life

OTHER BOOKS BY CAITLIN O'CONNELL:

The Elephant's Secret Sense: The Hidden Life of the Wild Herds of Africa

The Elephant Scientist

AN ELEPHANT'S LIFE

AN INTIMATE PORTRAIT FROM AFRICA

CAITLIN O'CONNELL

Photography by Caitlin O'Connell and Timothy Rodwell

LYONS PRESS

Guilford, Connecticut

An imprint of Globe Pequot Press

To buy books in quantity for corporate use
or incentives, call **(800) 962-0973**
or e-mail **premiums@GlobePequot.com.**

Lyons Press is an imprint of Globe Pequot Press.

Text design: Sheryl Pirolo Kober
Layout artist: Melissa Evarts
Project editor: Gregory Hyman

Interior photos by Caitlin O'Connell and Timothy Rodwell unless otherwise noted.
Map © Footprint Handbooks. Design by Maryann Dube.

Library of Congress Cataloging-in-Publication Data is available on file.

ISBN 978-0-7627-6374-0

Printed in China

10 9 8 7 6 5 4 3 2

In great appreciation to my parents, Dan and Aline O'Connell, for my early exposure to the natural world within the wilds of New Jersey. And a special thanks to Dad, whose passion for photography was contagious.

—Caitlin O'Connell

In loving memory of my mother and father, Margaret and David Rodwell, who gave me my first taste of wild Africa.

—Tim Rodwell

Contents

Introduction ix

Chapter 1: On Location 1

Chapter 2: Family Life 35

Chapter 3: A Baby Is Born 75

Chapter 4: The Adolescent Bull 103

Chapter 5: The Boys' Club 125

Chapter 6: Sex in Bull City 151

Chapter 7: The End of a Reign 171

Chapter 8: Camp Life 181

Afterword 185

Photographer's Note 186

Acknowledgments 190

About the Author and Photographers 193

INTRODUCTION

It's not every day that one is offered a once-in-a-lifetime opportunity, but when my husband Tim and I were given the chance to study nature's largest land creature in Africa, we jumped at it. It was a life-changing moment—one that I'll never regret.

I have been studying elephants for almost twenty years now, and there is never a dull moment, never an experience from which I don't learn something new about the elephant and about myself (including just how much heat, dust, and sand in the teeth and on my camera lens I can tolerate). I always feel like a privileged insider within the elephant's world.

I put together this collection of elephant images that Tim and I took over the course of my research at Mushara waterhole in Etosha National Park, Namibia, in the hope of helping you see the elephant and its world from that same insider perspective—to witness those first social steps, or missteps, of the calf, the heartwarming dedication of a matriarch, the stunning displays of ritual, the tribulations of a young male leaving his family, the ways in which dominance plays out, the testosterone-fueled state of musth males looking for a mate, the fierce protection offered by a best buddy, as well as the heart-wrenching reunions of a family.

Some stunning collections of elephant photos have appeared in books in recent years, but most of these collections consist of a series of individual photographs that record disconnected moments in time, with no real sense of an elephant's life as it progresses from beginning to end. It struck me that a photo book could be an opportunity to do just that—illustrate an elephant's life, moment by moment. In this book, I demonstrate typical, and sometimes not-so-typical elephant behavior by capturing an event in the moment, through illustrative sequences of dynamic photographs that allow the event to be experienced visually rather than just through words or isolated snapshots.

I also wanted to highlight the fact that elephants and other highly intelligent animals have rituals very similar to our own. Although we can never know for sure the extent of some rituals' meaning, and in order to avoid approaching anthropomorphism, I simply suggest that elephants might serve as a reminder that we as human beings are not so unique in our social complexity as we sometimes like to think.

An Elephant's Life proceeds chronologically, from the birth of the calf to the coming-of-age bull to the wounding of the dominant bull (in this case, a bull named Greg) at the height of his reign. I have tried to present the science—what we know, suspect, or still wonder about—in a way that enriches but doesn't overwhelm the experience of the images. Although this volume is not meant to be a comprehensive treatment, I have picked out some defining moments in an elephant's life to share with you, up close and personal, with the hope that you enjoy the experience and perhaps gain new insight into the majesty, the joy, and even sometimes the pain of an elephant's life.

SUSAN MCCONNELL

Between the vantage point of a tower and a bunker, we've learned a great deal about elephants through many, many hours of patient observation in sometimes not so comfortable conditions. But as you can see, it's hard to pass up the opportunity to get so close to the action, despite the occasional bits of dung blown into your face with a sudden gust of wind.

CHAPTER 1

On Location

THE RESEARCH

My elephant research began in Etosha National Park, Namibia, in 1992, when my husband, Tim, and I were contracted by the Namibian Ministry of Environment and Tourism and invited to undertake a study of elephants. Although not elephant specialists at the time, we were dedicated field scientists who happened to be in the right place at the right time when the opportunity arose.

Our mission was broad. We were to track movements of elephants within the Okavango River Delta, a system that extends through the Caprivi region of Namibia and into Zambia, Zimbabwe, and Angola.

While tracking the elephants, we were to document every aspect of the animals' complex social lives, from their demographics to their communications. Finally, we were assigned the task of monitoring any flare-ups in the ongoing conflict between elephants and the local people who had to share the land and its resources. It was a daunting task with a three-year timeline.

Early on in the research, when I was able to spend the winters in Etosha National Park where we could download satellite tracking information from collared elephants, I made my first observations about how elephants communicate. These findings launched my decade-long investigation into the way sound waves travel in elephants' environments and the ability of elephants to detect both acoustic and seismic information. The advantage of detecting the seismic components of elephant vocalizations was seeing that elephants had the potential to communicate over larger distances than previously thought; it also meant they had an additional channel of communication via signals detected through their feet and trunks. In the late 1990s, while finishing my PhD research at the University of California, Davis, I received a Rotary International Vocational Fellowship that enabled me to return to Namibia to test some of my ideas and to build on my previous research into elephant communication, as well as to search for ways to reduce elephant-human conflict. Around this time, my mentor, Lynette Hart; a geophysicist colleague, Byron Arnason; and I were able to demonstrate that elephant vocalizations indeed propagate in the ground with distinct properties from airborne waves.

After receiving a grant from the National Geographic Society and the U.S. Fish and Wildlife Service as well as a Bio-X Interdisciplinary postdoctoral fellowship at Stanford University, I was able to return to my field site at Mushara waterhole in the early to mid-2000s heading a team of researchers specializing in behavior, geophysics, and geography. Over several seasons, we succeeded in demonstrating that my hypothesis was indeed correct—that not only do low-frequency elephant vocalizations (in the range of 20 hertz, which is below the threshold of human hearing) propagate through the ground, but that other elephants are able to detect and interpret this information at a considerable distance through their feet.

It was during this time—when I had more team members to help me document other aspects of an elephant's social life—that we started to build an identification system and to develop detailed records of both male and female elephants, their identifying features, their family members and extended associates, as well as their social status within groups. Some of these characters, such as Big Momma and Greg, will be highlighted in the upcoming chapters.

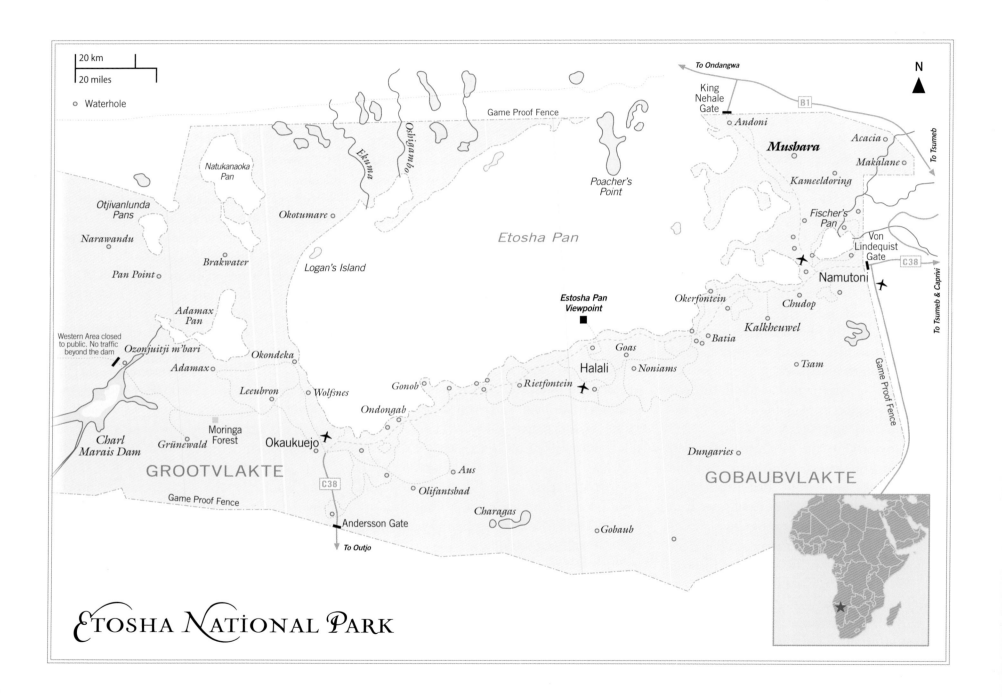

ETOSHA NATIONAL PARK

20 km
20 miles

○ Waterhole

To Ondangwa
King Nehale Gate
Andoni
Mushara
Acacia
Makalane
Kameeldoring
Fischer's Pan
Von Lindequist Gate
Namutoni
To Tsumeb
To Tsumeb & Caprivi
C38

Game Proof Fence

Natukanaoka Pan

Poacher's Point

Etosha Pan

Otjivanlunda Pans
Okotumare
Narawandu
Brakwater
Logan's Island

Okerfontein
Chudop

Estosha Pan Viewpoint
Kalkheuwel

Pan Point
Adamax Pan
Batia
Goas
Tsam

Western Area closed to public. No traffic beyond the dam
Ozonjuitji m'bari
Okondeka
Noniams

Adamax
Halali
Rietfontein
Leeubron
Wolfsnes
Gonob
Ondongab

Charl Marais Dam
Grünewald
Moringa Forest
Okaukuejo
Aus
Dungaries

GROOTVLAKTE
C38
Olifantsbad
GOBAUBVLAKTE

Game Proof Fence
Charagas
Gobaub

Andersson Gate
To Outjo

With more observers and a growing record of known elephant individuals, we started to notice the males exhibiting more and more unexpected behaviors. Much of the pioneering work on elephant behavior had been based on long-term studies of herds headed by matriarchs, which consisted of elephant cows of various ages and juveniles and calves of both sexes. The lives of mature bull elephants were relatively poorly understood, at least in terms of what was published.

After many seasons at Mushara, my colleagues and I are now filling in the blanks. For example, bull groups do not appear to be made up of casual associates or single "best buddies," as previously described, but rather of several members who share a close bond. Some of these bonds persist over years, though we also observe larger groups that form, split up, and re-form, in a phenomenon known to elephant scientists as "fission-fusion" and seen in previous studies of matriarchal herds. These fission-fusion dynamics appear to be influenced by environmental factors, particularly rainfall, which determines the amount of available drinking water.

What we've seen is a clear hierarchy that exists among bulls within our study population. Bulls have access to the best drinking spots and the cleanest water according to their social rank. Every visit to the watering hole by a group of bulls is an opportunity for us to mine a rich data set. In order to understand how the hierarchy is structured, we keep score every time a bull successfully displaces another bull from the favored drinking spot at our field site. We document which bulls are displaced and which bulls do the displacing using a Noldus Observer data logger, and we back up the real-time data with video logs. From this data, we are able to construct a hierarchy of bulls that we call the dominance matrix data grid based on scores of these aggressive contests.

The Environment

In June 1992, after my first night at Okaukuejo waterhole at the main tourist camp in Etosha National Park, my thirst for exploring Africa took on a different form. It turned from desire into a disquieting hunger, a persistent and anxious need for more. Seeing wild elephants in this stark desert context for the first time changed the course of my personal and professional life. There was something about seeing these great ghostly giants in the open desert coming and going silently throughout the night that made me want to understand the rhythm of Africa on a more personal level. I no longer wanted to be a tourist, a bystander in this amazingly intact land that was still so wild and full of life.

Proclaimed a game reserve in 1907 by German governor Frederich von Lindequist, Etosha was originally a bit more than 90,000 square kilometers (nearly 35,000 square miles), incorporating the massive extinct lake Etosha Pan, spanning 4,590 kilometers (2,852 miles). The size of the park fluctuated over the next century, the current area covering just over 22,000 square kilometers (8,494 square miles) and hosting 114 mammal species—such as elephants, rhinos, giraffe, zebra, wildebeest, kudu, lions, and leopards—and 340 bird species, over 100 reptiles, 16 amphibians, and one fish species.

The park is relatively flat except for rocky escarpments in the west that are closed to tourism. Much of the rest of the park ranges in habitat from vast grass plains and shrubs surrounding the pan to deciduous trees, consisting of mopane trees and what is called mixed bushveld. The bushveld ranges from dense bush to open tree savannahs (including many acacia species) to the sandy environment of the northeast called the tree sandveld, where tree species tend to grow taller in the deep sand. Our field site, Mushara, is named after the terminalia species predominant in the area.

The Camp and Field Site

The Mushara field camp is a temporary, seasonal 30 by 30-foot canvas enclosure surrounding a three-story, 20-foot-high permanent tower positioned 240 feet from the waterhole. The entire perimeter of the camp is enclosed by an electric fence.

Etosha Pan is an expansive dry lake bed that sometimes floods in the wet season. Over the course of our studies, 2004, 2005, and 2007 were dry years (around 300 mm of rain) and 2006, 2008, and 2009 were relatively wet years (more than 500 mm of rain). We found that the difference in rainfall between years correlated with male elephant group sizes—the drier years having much bigger group sizes than the wetter years. It appears that the environment has an influence on sociality in this region, which may suggest that elephants have a slightly different social organization in arid environments than they do in environments with perennial rivers and higher rainfall. If this is true, then it is all the more important to conduct long-term research on elephant social structure in different environments to understand the variation in their social dynamics and complexity across their range.

Every year from 2002 to the present, we have returned to Mushara during the dry months of June and July, when elephants come to the waterholes in great numbers. At the height of the dry season, drinking water is scarce, and the water at Mushara draws elephants and other wildlife. During this time, we have been monitoring bonded male groups to determine their social structure and to find out what holds these groups together.

Facing page: Etosha pan floods seasonally and is normally dry in the dry season (top). The pan flooded in 2006 after a fifty-year-high rainfall and remained full in the dry season (bottom).

The base camp has a kitchen, dining area, pantry, two-person field tent, outhouse and solar shower, as well as an elephant dung processing facility at the base of the tower, a changing area, and an exercise space. The electrical needs of the research and camp operation are run off a solar panel that charges a bank of 12-volt batteries.

The first platform level of the tower holds three two-person tents, and the second level contains the research operation, where elephant identifications are made, behavior data are collected, fecal samples are mapped, and behavior sessions are recorded with a video camera. The third level of the tower has an additional two-person tent, a year-round operated remote camera trap, and it is where the playback and acoustic experiments are conducted and vocalizations are recorded.

In addition to the research area on the second floor of the tower, outside the electrical fence there is a small seven-by-seven-foot cement bunker sixty feet from the waterhole that allows for closer observations and elephant identification work. Just to the right of the bunker, seismic playback equipment is buried in the ground and audio equipment is hidden underneath a pile of thorny branches, surrounded by calcrete rocks to protect the equipment from curious elephants and lions. All of this equipment is controlled remotely from the tower with wires buried between the tower and the branch pile.

If you don't mind roughing it, our field camp at Mushara is a five-star animal experience within an exclusive resort. By day, you can enjoy breathtaking views of an animal Garden of Eden, with wildlife enough to fill several arks. The crowned and blacksmith plovers patrol the shores, making the pan seem like a vast lake, harkening back to prehistoric times when Etosha Pan was a permanent lake.

On any given day, breakfast is served at 8 a.m. with enough time for students to finish preparing dung samples from the previous day, and perhaps a postcard or two before the elephant bulls tend to stroll in at about 10:30 a.m. On busy bull days, visits tend to occur on and off throughout the day, with the longer sessions lasting up to several hours and sometimes involving more than twenty bulls. On less busy days, there may only be two to three bulls coming in to drink over the course of the day.

In and around these elephant data collection sessions, team members rotate through a roster of kitchen and camp duties, and those on lunch duty juggle between their research responsibilities and preparing food for the team. Lunch on the research deck is always a treat, whether we are entertained by an ostrich mating ritual, a host of vultures coming in to drink after dining on the remains of the local lion pride's kill from the night before, or a group of bulls cooling off with a mud bath.

Sometime after 4 p.m., if there are any family groups in the area, they start to arrive for a drink. If we are lucky enough, they arrive with enough remaining afternoon light for a few team members to get into the bunker for close-up photo identifications, while the rest of the team documents the visit with video, scoring dominance interactions within and between family groups.

THE RESEARCH TEAM AT WORK

Over the years, we have compiled a detailed identification book cataloging each elephant and its distinctive features, such as ear tears and holes, tail hair pattern, tusk shape, and overall size. This allows us to identify individuals and keep track of changes of any features over time, such as a broken tusk, a new tear in the ear, missing tail hair, or the arrival of a new baby, and whether and for how long a resident bull or matriarch does not show up from season to season.

We keep a database of behaviors and group dynamics using a Noldus Observer data logger and video logs to document all interactions in real time while elephants visit the waterhole. Our other work at Mushara has us keeping track of the female-headed herds. We record new births as well as the departures of the coming-of-age bulls, and note how dominance within and between family groups appears to shape certain interactions. As with the bulls, much of the drama within and between herds centers on access to water.

At the same time, we collect dung samples from these events in order to analyze levels of stress hormones, specifically cortisol, throughout the field season. Fecal samples from bulls are tested for testosterone levels during aggressive interactions or to confirm when a bull is in the hormonal state of musth—a period similar to rutting in antelope, when a male becomes more reproductively active. Since it takes twenty-four hours for relevant hormones to show up in the dung, the potential impact of behaviors witnessed on one day will only show up in fecal samples collected on the following day. Collecting elephant dung has also allowed us to see whether (and how) bonded bulls are related genetically, which we hope will result in some interesting findings. We also use equipment to make acoustic and seismic recordings of elephant vocalizations. Studying elephants' reactions to the recordings (known as a playback study) has been an ongoing focus of the research.

THE DENIZENS OF MUSHARA

Aside from elephants, many other animals rely on Mushara waterhole at the northeast corner of the park, as it is one of the very few places to drink in the dry season. Zebra, giraffe, oryx, springbok, eland, and kudu rely on Mushara, as do their predators—the lions, jackals, and hyenas.

It can be a little nerve-racking to live on the lion's dinner plate over the course of the field season, but we conduct our research activities with caution and are always on the lookout for a lion on the prowl. Most of the time their antics are quite entertaining, whether they be the ardent efforts of a lioness to get her suitor to perform yet one more time (apparently, as many as a thousand copulations are necessary for ovulation to occur), making for a very noisy night, or the failed attempts of Bobtail's subadult sons at hunting.

Although Mushara can be quite chaotic with so many different species vying for a position at the water, some sunsets are so quiet that all that can be heard are the beating wings and chortling of the double-banded sand grouse while a few lone gemsbok take an evening drink.

After dark, Mushara transforms. The air is crisp, and nocturnal sounds announce the evening, starting with a jackal chorus. Depending on the phase of the moon, the landscape is glowing in the moonlight or the black sky is lit up with a brilliant path of stars.

Aerial view of Mushara tower and research camp. Mushara waterhole is a natural spring; the flow is controlled by a ball valve. The spring flows into a trough and then spills over into a shallow clay depression, or pan. The head of the trough holds the freshest water, so access to this spot is often coveted by dominant elephants. The square cement bunker to the right of the waterhole allows us a close (and safe) vantage for observations and ID work.

Okaukuejo waterhole with bull elephant

Our Mushara field camp is a temporary, seasonal 30 by 30-foot canvas enclosure surrounding a three-story, 20-foot-high permanent tower. The entire perimeter of the camp is enclosed by an electric fence to keep out unwanted visitors.

My team and I jump into action as soon as a family group arrives after sunset. Low light binoculars and night vision gear are used to count the group as they come in. We also record everything on a video camera attached to a night vision system.

The field team observes elephant activity at the waterhole with night vision equipment. At the same time, we use red light headlamps (facing page, bottom left) to conduct behavioral research with minimal disturbance to the animals.

Although the nighttime activity can get very exciting with a lot of family groups visiting, it can also be hard on the team after a whole day of watching the bulls and with the temperature dropping as the hours go by. Everyone looks forward to a good night's sleep in a warm sleeping bag after these nights.

After collection, fecal samples for hormone analysis are dried for twenty-four hours in individual baskets within our solar-powered dung dryer. Each sample is then sifted and fecal powder is stored for later radioimmunoassay treatment to extract hormones. Here (top left), field assistant Tanya Meyer prepares to sift a sample in the least windy place she can find—which happens to be in the back of the truck. Genetic information on certain individuals is obtained by collecting fecal samples in which cells from the colon have sloughed off and DNA can be extracted (bottom left). Students Andrew Wicklund and Mary Thurber (above) study how hormones from known fecal samples degrade over time.

In addition to the research area on the second floor of the tower at base camp, there is a small cement bunker (shown in the foreground here) that allows for closer observation of the elephants. In the safety of the tower, I show my student, Mindi Summers, how to identify the bulls at the waterhole using a book which records ear tears, tail hair patterns and other defining characteristics. Meanwhile, Mindi has the behavior datalogger on a tablet PC open, ready to enter behaviors that I call out to her.

Inside the bunker, I have had some hairy moments alone when a long, wrinkly trunk has suddenly appeared in the viewing slit. On more than one occasion, a dripping proboscis has practically knocked over my tripod and assaulted me with heavy breathing and bad breath, like a giant worm testing, assessing what lies within that cement box. I've had to stretch myself well out of the way lest the brain attached to this brawn were to decide to do something more than just investigate. There is also a moment of morbid fascination, time standing still, as an elephant comes full steam ahead in a charge, with no sign of stopping. Females are more likely to follow through with a charge than males, because they often have babies to protect. Fortunately, in this case I was able to retreat into the concrete bunker and let this wary young female, Panga (above), drink in peace with her family.

Because hind foot length scales with shoulder height and age, my graduate student (and general curator of the Oakland Zoo), Colleen Kinzley, and I measure as many of the known male footprints as we can so that we can get a better age estimate than just measuring shoulder height (which we do with a laser altimeter back in the tower).

Herds of zebra, as well as other animals, rely on the water at Mushara.

Facing page: Bobtail and her four cubs.

It can be a little nerve-racking to live on the lion's dinner plate, but we conduct our research activities with caution and are always on the lookout for a lion on the prowl. Now that Bobtail's sons are growing up, some of their antics can be quite entertaining to watch.

As the lion is the primary predator of elephants, female elephants are usually very intolerant of lions' presence at a waterhole, particularly if there are new calves in the group. Such intolerance is not usually demonstrated by adult bull elephants, who rarely acknowledge the presence of lions at a waterhole unless they are in their path, in which case the bull will simply toss his trunk to get rid of the menace. Every so often, a younger bull will respond more aggressively, as if he remembers what it was like to live inside the family that is plagued by lions on the prowl; perhaps he may even have been stalked by a brave pride when distancing himself from his family. In the photo sequence on pages 27–29, Keith catches Bobtail's subadult sons off guard and charges them quite aggressively, kicking up sand with his foot, shaking his head in warning, and tossing his trunk to hurry them on their way, without hesitation.

During our safaris between Mushara and the closest waterhole, Kameeldoring, occasionally we found ourselves in the middle of a feud between the pride of lions that is trying to claim Kameeldoring as their territory and the group in flux at Mushara, whose range extends to Kameeldoring. One day, when we were finished with our photo shoot of the feud, I pulled away, only to realize that we had a flat tire and had to change it in the middle of lion country before it got dark, or face having to sleep in the vehicle that night. This is a good example of why it is so important that a field vehicle have at least one working spare tire.

In addition to elephants, Etosha National Park hosts 114 mammal species—such as rhinos, giraffe, zebra, wildebeest, kudu, lions, and leopards—and 340 bird species, more than 100 reptiles, 16 amphibians, and one fish species.

Whenever elephants are not present, there is always a photographic moment to be had with other animals throughout the day but especially at sunrise and sunset.

A few gemsbok take a drink at sunset.

CHAPTER 2

Family Life

Female elephants live much of their lives separately from adult males and within extended social networks, the core of which are called family groups. A mother, grandmother, and maybe even a great-grandmother live together with daughters, nieces, granddaughters, and their offspring—totaling, on average, about fifteen individuals that remain together for life. These core family groups have close ties with related and more distantly related bond groups that are seen less frequently. Extensions of these bond groups are called clans.

THE MATRIARCH

The matriarch, the oldest female (sometimes in the range of sixty years old or over) in the family group, is the most important member of the extended elephant family. She makes decisions about where and when to move and rest, both on a daily and seasonal basis. Her memory is an important repository of knowledge and is key to the family's survival. When a group's matriarch becomes too ill or weak to lead, the next oldest female family member replaces her. The replacement leader is not necessarily the daughter or sister of the matriarch. The hierarchal social system of elephants emphasizes the importance of age and experience over kinship.

Each matriarch has a different approach to her task of leadership, as evident in her response to a potentially dangerous situation. I've seen matriarchs that charge first and ask questions later, others that take a more defensive approach, and still others that approach a potential danger as a curiosity.

For example, Big Momma casually assesses my presence with ears held out, as seen in the photo on the facing page, but her head is not held up aggressively, nor are her feet planted firmly on the ground with legs straight to give her a larger appearance. Her posture immediately conveys that she is calm, cool, and collected. Her ears are extended, which indicates that she is indeed aware of my presence, but they are not particularly stiff, and her trunk is completely flaccid, indicating that my presence is not a threat to her. Sure, she could reach over and whack me with that trunk and even kill me with the blow, but she doesn't indicate any such intention. She appears more curious than aggressive.

The easiest way to identify Big Momma is to look for the raised bump in the middle of her right ear, her extremely large ears, and her short scimitar tusks. Since Big Momma exhibits such calm confidence, we've been watching her offspring to see if her character is passed on to the next generation.

The character of the matriarch can define the character of the group as a whole. As such, there is a clear pecking order among family groups that is dependent on the status of the matriarch within the larger population.

Body posture reveals much about an elephant's character. Among the adult females of Big Momma's group, some are more aggressive and outgoing in their displays of aggression than Big Momma, who is passive and confident in her approach and posture. One such member is Nandi, a young, particularly aggressive female often witnessed in various threatening postures. Another female our team often saw acting aggressively was Sheba.

In this photo, Nandi holds her ears straight out in threatening posture. Nandi has long, slender straight tusks and a small c-shaped cutout in the middle of the edge of the right ear. On the facing page, note the first elephant on the left with the noticeable square tab in the middle edge of her right ear. This is Sheba. Along with her contemporary Panga (missing her left tusk), she appears in this series of photographs displaying a lot of aggressive posturing.

Sheba is positioned in an aggressive posture with her ears held out, facing me as I take her photo from the bunker. She is unsure and very wary of my presence.

If I didn't have the protection of the bunker, Sheba could charge. And when a female charges, it's usually not a mock charge. They mean business. Since they are protecting young, they tend to be much more dangerous and volatile than male elephants.

Shaka, a coming-of-age male in Big Momma's family, arrives at the waterhole ahead of the rest of the group, showing his first signs of independence. Breaking away from the family can take several years before a male is fully independent.

Born just before our 2010 field season, these two new additions to Big Momma's family are part of a baby boom as a result of a very good wet season in 2008. They are not allowed to stray too far without a mother's protective trunk reining them in.

Big Momma's family comes to Mushara for a drink in the late afternoon. Used to my presence in the bunker, they show no sign of distress, but when the younger, more defensive females pass, they make sure I know they are aware of me.

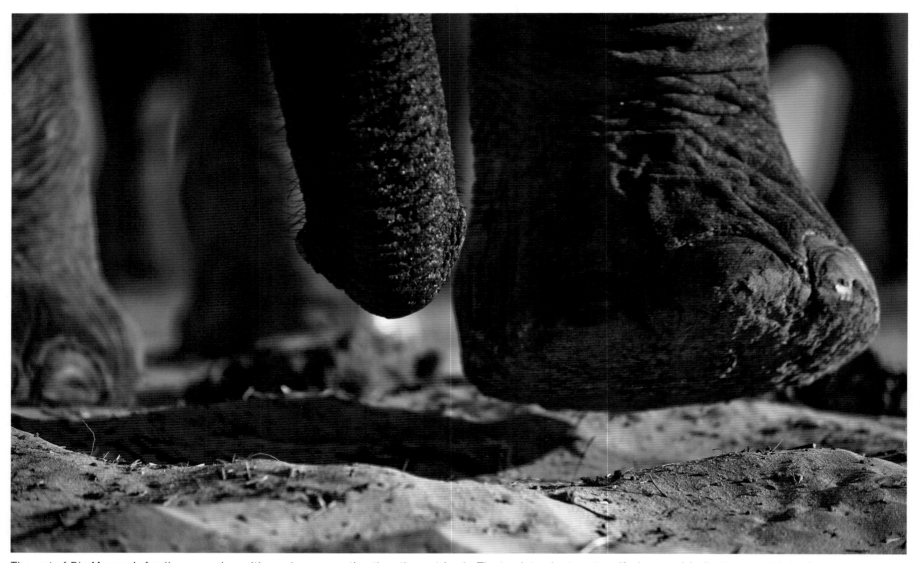

The rest of Big Momma's family approaches with much more caution than the matriarch. The trunk-to-chest gesture (facing page) indicates uncertainty about my presence in the bunker in front of the waterhole. Sometimes, when an elephant is uncertain, it will place its weight forward on its feet and literally tip-toe, rather than walk with more confidence and more weight placed on the footpad first, then toe as Big Momma does upon entry to the waterhole.

An Elephant's Life

Does a mother's character get passed on to the next generation? Note Big Momma and her calm calf (above right) compared to the more aggressive mother and calf on the facing page (heads raised and ears held out) and the hesitant mother and her tentative calf (above left).

Big Momma (note the bump on her ear) and Nandi (on Big Momma's right) see that a young bull is in trouble. He has fallen into the drinking trough, which has steep walls that make it very difficult for a baby to climb out. The two females try to lift the calf out of the trough. Here and in the photos that follow, they resort to getting onto their knees in a coordinated effort to get underneath him and hoist him to safety.

After kneeling down to scoop the calf up with her trunk, Big Momma (above left) continues to apply pressure as the calf's mom (Nandi on facing page) pulls him up by the rump.

Now out of immediate danger, the sopping young bull rests with his rescuers. When such traumatic events occur, it's often a big sister who steps in to provide a comforting trunk.

Life at the Waterhole

Predators are a constant threat, and lions that might hesitate to tackle an elephant during times of plenty can be emboldened during the dry season. When lions are in the area, the fear of predation is palpable in the family's wary approach to water. But when the family is relaxed, their play—cavorting in the water, dusting, and sparring—makes for wonderful entertainment. Bathing helps to cool elephants in the heat of the day. Mudding and dusting are an important part of an elephant's skin care as the caked-on mud and dust are then rubbed off, along with many skin parasites.

A family enjoys a favorite dusting spot. By rolling around and blowing dust, the youngsters make the ritual fun—though it also has an important function. With mud caked on, an elephant can rub against a tree to remove parasites.

Hierarchies at Work

Family life isn't always peaceful at the waterhole, however. Given the pandemonium of three, four, and sometimes five herds arriving at the waterhole at the same time (which can amount to more than two hundred elephants), it is fascinating to see that there is a clear pecking order among the family groups. The pushing, shoving, and posturing to access the source of the artesian well, and thus the best quality water, is striking.

Dominance plays a key role in elephant society. Dominance hierarchies are thought to form in animal populations to minimize conflict over resources, such as food, water, and mates. Researchers have shown that female elephants form dominance hierarchies, both within and between family groups. We can observe these hierarchies in the way that elephants compete for access to water, particularly the cleanest water, which at Mushara is the outflow of the spring that flows to the head of a cement trough.

The aggression shown by some matriarchs toward others may seem surprising, particularly when it appears to a human onlooker that there is plenty of room for all to drink. When the stakes are high—such as when gaining access to scarce water and defending the family against predators—rank and coalitions become apparent.

Elephants have been known to form coalitions to protect valuable resources, such as water—a tactic used successfully by other species as well. When a newcomer approaches a water hole already claimed by a group, a coalition of individuals may attempt to intimidate the newcomer.

On very hot days, there's a traffic jam at Mushara waterhole and elephants have to make their way through the other animals to get to the water. In this photo, a coming-of-age male (on the left-hand side of this page) towers over the rest of his family.

Despite their need for a drink, this thirsty family heads toward the trough containing fresh spring water rather than drinking from the muddy pan. After a long drink and mud bath, the family dusts themselves with sand. Covering their muddy bodies with sand helps to protect their skin from parasites. This is a time for play and rest as the youngster (facing page, on the left) does a face plant into a favorite dusting hole.

A family enters at dusk. Family groups tend to arrive at a waterhole from late afternoon to dusk. Air temperatures drop at dusk, creating favorable conditions for sound transmission, which means that elephants can communicate better at this time, and therefore might better coordinate movements and perhaps feel more secure approaching the water when predators are on the prowl.

The waterhole is very social and an important place for youngsters in extended families to meet, play, spar, and bond, perhaps providing important foundations for friendships later in life. At sunset, adult males may also be at the waterhole, which means that the younger bulls still within their families get a chance to interact with adult males in a friendly setting. Some older bulls solicit such interaction, whereas others don't show much interest and leave the area just as the families arrive, unless there is a female in estrus. Then the adult bulls will take an interest and stay longer to inspect the females and socialize.

On one particular occasion three groups—the Left Hook, Left Tusker, and Crooked Tail families—arrived at the waterhole at the same time. A clearly defined seniority became evident as the groups lined up for their turn to drink. Left Hook's family (we identify Left Hook by her short and outwardly splayed left tusk) was first to the trough but was quickly displaced by Left Tusker (who has no right tusk) and her family (the group in the foreground), which occupied the favored spot at the head of the trough unchallenged throughout their visit. Last came the Crooked Tails (most of whom we identify by their short, twisted tails), who were displaced all the way around the pan and forced to stand in the southeast clearing, huddled and rumbling until it was their turn. When Left Tusker finally departed, Left Hook took back command of the head of the trough, leaving the Crooked Tail clan to go downstream, until finally Left Hook left the scene and the Crooked Tails occupied the head.

There is a strict hierarchy between matriarchs and their family groups, with stiff competition for access to the best water at Mushara. Depending on their ranking, it can take as little as a trunk throw to send a thirsty family on its way.

Big Momma and her family want to defend their right to access their waterhole, but the newcomer (near left) is having none of it and marches toward her challengers with ears held out. As we watch, the four elephants, led by Big Momma, stand shoulder to shoulder in a line, with their ears outstretched to intimidate the newcomer.

The young newcomer matriarch (near left) breaks Big Momma's lineup (on right) without much effort.

Despite Big Momma's surprising show of aggression and the intimidating phalanx of females, the new female holds her ground. Given that she is probably younger than Big Momma (judging from her height and back length) and some of Big Momma's formidable cohorts, her resistance is particularly surprising.

Big Momma's coalition members sense defeat and turn tail.

AN ELEPHANT'S LIFE

In a second attempt, Big Momma's family forms a more aggressive line (bottom) and Big Momma charges the intruder with her trunk in a tight fist, dragging it on the ground and then throwing it at the water-hogging tyrant. I have never seen one female challenge another so aggressively and was sure Big Momma would send the newcomer off without a contest.

After a few tense moments, the newcomer charges the already retreating lineup, thereby scattering Big Momma's coalition.

To show the seriousness of her intent, the newcomer tusks a coalition member in the backside as she flees to safety.

After being displaced, Big Momma's family members hang their heads in defeat and walk off to a safe distance, waiting in the wings until the new queen and her family have had their fill and leave. So much for the coalition's efforts to defend its turf. Despite their loss, the strategy they used is known to be effective for many species, particularly primates and female elephants elsewhere in Africa, and maybe for Big Momma, too—on another day with another challenger. As soon as Big Momma approaches her family to reunite after her defeat by the newcomer, a most compelling ritual ensues. The family starts roaring and rumbling and flapping their ears, urinating and defecating in greeting as they encircle their matriarch, who approaches with her trunk outstretched to greet her family after only minutes of separation. Clearly such situations of defeat and separation are highly traumatic for females. And yet the intensity of this reunion is very similar to greetings I have witnessed after a short foraging separation. Family members don't like to be separated even under the best of circumstances.

Together again, Big Momma and her family return to the waterhole, prepared to drink when deemed their turn.

All matriarchs have to negotiate their position at the waterhole upon first approach. Some are more commanding in their demeanor and succeed in supplanting the family already present. Although Big Momma is a very dominant matriarch, she does not use such tactics, and as such, sometimes prefers the sideline to combat, and yet still commands the respect and dominance on most occasions.

CHAPTER 3

A Baby Is Born

Under the watchful eye of its mother, older siblings, and aunts, a young elephant calf learns important lessons about food, social boundaries, ritual, and danger, all while enjoying the frivolities of youth. After a gestation period of about twenty-two months, a baby is born weighing about 250 pounds and is on the move very shortly thereafter. A baby elephant is able to keep up with its family on small but sturdy legs. Only its trunk muscles need time to mature.

For the first few months of life, the trunk hangs flaccid, a seemingly perplexing appendage that doesn't perform for the calf as it does for other family members, which appears to cause young elephants some confusion.

One of the first things the calf learns to do with its trunk is to place the tip in another family member's mouth in ritual greeting. Over the next few weeks and months the baby adds to his repertoire such trunk skills as smelling, browsing, dusting, wrestling, and drinking. Another important use of the trunk is to keep tabs on mom through touch and smell. Despite all of the trunk's versatility, a baby suckles with its mouth—a task that poses challenges for the baby of a very tall mother.

Calves under a year old still fit under their mother's belly—a useful rule of thumb for researchers recording the age of elephants.

The Importance of Ritual

Nothing says ritual to an elephant more than sparring and the trunk-to-mouth greeting. These two rituals are a very important part of growing up and are learned at a very young age. For a male, sparring becomes a test of strength, will, and keeping one's cool. The trunk-to-mouth greeting is a gesture of acknowledgment, mutual respect, and—from a younger elephant to an older elephant—maybe even a sign of reverence. For the less dominant bull, it seems to serve as an acknowledgment of a higher-ranking individual's seniority and makes it clear at the beginning of a drinking bout who is in charge. In some situations the elephant trunk-to-mouth greeting appears to serve as an invitation for further social interaction or as a bonding gesture among reunited individuals. The trunk-to-mouth greeting is an important gesture that reinforces bonds within the family, as well as between families and extended bond groups.

Boy Trouble

For the African elephant, there are particular challenges to growing up male. The pre-adolescent male pushes boundaries on all fronts—picking fights with the wrong guy, play-mounting his sister, and even chasing other wildlife. Inevitably, his mother and aunts come to the rescue when he finds himself in trouble.

Bonds form between juvenile bulls from extended family groups early on, and these young males seek safety in numbers, often arriving at a waterhole on their own, well before reinforcements show up in the form of their families. Sometimes these males are poorly behaved, particularly if there is a very young female in estrus. They can take on the traits of a marauding gang.

Male elephants typically leave their family groups when they reach sexual maturity, at about age fourteen (between twelve and fifteen on average). They then begin spending time with other bulls their age. Each bull often joins a group of bonded older bulls.

A baby elephant suckles from its mother with its mouth rather than its trunk. We are able to identify the calves that are less than a year old because they are still able to fit under their mother's belly when nursing.

Babies within the family that are born within months of each other are bound to form very close bonds.

The elephant calf on the facing page can hold its trunk straight out in front of its body to smell something unusual (like me) in the bunker. At about two years old, an elephant's tusks (which are incisors) start to protrude, with a male elephant's tusks growing faster than those of his sisters, until eventually a male's tusks are much wider and often longer than the female's. The elephant on this page is just developing trunk dexterity.

The ritual of sparring is learned from a very early age (facing page) as is the ritual trunk-to-mouth greeting (this page) even when the trunk can't quite reach an elder's mouth.

The trunk-to-mouth greeting is one of the earliest gestures a baby elephant learns. It is a sign of acknowledgment, mutual respect, and social bonding.

A mother elephant uses her trunk to guide her baby away from potential danger. As if unconvinced of the danger of my proximity, the baby places its trunk in its mouth, which appears to signal uncertainty.

This little bull is pretty certain of the potential threat to his family that my presence has created, and he approaches with ears out and head up, using his trunk to get a better whiff of his suspect.

Pre-adolescent male elephants often push boundaries on all fronts. Here a male calf does so by play-mounting his sister. But an older sister (facing page) comes to the rescue and pushes him off with her trunk when she catches him being naughty.

The bullying among young elephants can start early. Here a slightly older calf pulls a baby's trunk (facing page), while the onlookers seem to want to join in the game.

Big Momma steps in to quell the roughhousing.

Once Big Momma appears, the troublemaker drops the baby's trunk.

Young bulls from large families enjoy getting to meet up with and interact with older bulls present at the waterhole. Adult bulls don't seem to like the chaos of families drinking, so sometimes the youngsters only get a few minutes to say hello to the big boys before the adults move off.

As young bulls grow, so does their confidence. This young bull (left) is full of bravado, holding his head up and ears out, sweeping his trunk from side to side (even if it's just to clear the area of guinea fowl) as his family approaches the water. Often these very young bulls only have confidence as far as their line of sight allows. As soon as they can't see mom or other family members, they go bellowing after them so as not to be left alone. A few are braver and band together with other younger bulls to gain a sense of security through their buddies.

A bull calf has taken out his feistiness on his family, much to the dismay of mom. In this sequence, a young bull has taunted his siblings enough that his mother steps in to chase him off.

Young bulls seem to enjoy chasing other wildlife away from the waterhole.

Confident in the company of their buddies, young bulls sometimes stray much farther from their families than they would dare on their own. But when the dust settles, darkness sets in, and it comes time to catch up with relatives that have long since left the waterhole, they'll be the first to wail and carry on while running and trumpeting after their families.

An Elephant's Life

CHAPTER 4
The Adolescent Bull

Bulls between the age of twelve and fifteen leave their families when their quest for independence finally proves incompatible with a mother's mandate for peace. The severing of ties takes months to years and can be quite traumatic for young bulls raised in a tight-knit family.

Testosterone spikes in older teens are ordinarily kept in check by the presence of adult bulls in their midst, the elders suppressing high testosterone levels in the teens. When older bulls are removed from the social equation as a result of poaching, or when young bulls are reintroduced to a park without any adults, the young bulls can become a real menace, with results that are often sad. The lack of oversight from experienced bull elders can leave young bulls to run amok, committing violence against other elephants and other species.

One dramatic example of this phenomenon occurred in a private reserve in Pilansberg, South Africa, between 1992 and 1997. Adolescent bulls were relocated to this park from their native range after a selective harvest to keep numbers down in Kruger National Park in the 1980s. The young bulls were observed to experience initial musth at the age of eighteen, rather than around their mid-twenties.

These young bulls had been introduced to an area that was also home to a population of highly valued white rhinos relocated from elsewhere in South Africa. The stage was set for conflict, as elephants and rhinos are natural antagonists. Though rhinos are smaller, they are stubborn, and they tend not to back down when challenged by elephants, which, in turn, appears to provoke elephants greatly. Unchallenged by higher-ranking males, the younger elephants ended up attacking and killing forty rhinos before the decision was made that something had to be done to stop them.

Managers at the preserve decided to introduce six older bulls to see if they might somehow keep these teenagers in check. Upon the arrival of the older males, the younger ones instantly fell out of musth and stopped their delinquent behavior, thus providing clear evidence that the mere presence of older bulls suppresses the expression of testosterone in young bulls. And to further strengthen this theory, when the problem occurred in a second reserve in South Africa, it was solved in exactly the same way.

Although this problem was corrected by hormonal suppression, the resolution also suggested that young bulls might benefit from good male role models. Was something more than hormonal suppression at work? Did the younger bulls need social guidance and boundaries that older bulls provided in order for them to remain decent members of their society? A further study of this may provide valuable lessons for managing both captive elephants and bulls that are introduced to new parks and preserves. Humans might learn much from how nonhuman societies manage these vital interactions.

Even in Etosha National Park, young bulls can sometimes enter musth prematurely. During very wet years, when elephants have many drinking-site options, young bulls can wander and avoid close contact with older males—and they can thus fall outside the testosterone-suppressing presence of mature bulls. During such times, I have seen very young bulls enter into the hormonal state of musth years earlier than they would normally.

The ever-social Rocky Balboa (right) invites the young #112 (far right) for a spar with his trunk held high above the other's head. After many social interactions with other young bulls in 2010, #112 was given the name Speedy Gonzales, because of his habit of running to the waterhole to greet his compatriots, rather than sauntering in like many of the other young fellows. The young bulls are the hardest to name, because once they leave their families, they no longer have the association of several older females more easily identified by the nicks and tears in their ears and distinct body types. It takes time to first document defining features (which are usually very subtle) and then to witness their personalities for long enough to give them appropriate names. Because they may travel far and wide after leaving their families, we often don't see the same young bulls from one year to the next. This presents another challenge for naming them, as we feel we need to observe a bull at least three times before we can name him. Rocky Balboa got his name pretty quickly by his defining right hook (upcurved left tusk) and his affinity for sparring with bulls of all ages.

While the family drinks, a young bull approaches the bunker to see what's going on inside.

(Facing page) Young bulls will often play mount one another, either to show their dominance or to practice.

Here, teenage elephants are testing their own strength and practicing their sparring techniques, while blowing off a lot of steam in the process. On the facing page, Rocky Balboa, with his upcurved left tusk, is easily identified.

Neither of these two bulls seems to tire from their efforts nor does either of them show any sign of wanting to end the engagement, and, in the end, neither seems to be a clear winner. No doubt, this challenge will continue, maybe taking several years before dominance will be decided between them.

The confident teen Rocky Balboa takes on an older bull. The younger, smaller Rocky (on right in the photos above and on facing page), who we identify by his upcurved left tusk, tests the patience of this older bull who could easily put him in his place, but chooses to engage, perhaps to teach Rocky a gentle lesson about not setting his sights too high in a challenge.

After several wet years, Mushara had a baby boom. Following it, several young bulls were ousted a little earlier than they otherwise would have been (mother and calf on facing page, coming-of-age bull on this page). This mother shoves this young bull as she does not want him joining her family to drink. The young bull has tusk marks on his backside, indicating that this is not the first time he's been asked to leave by adult females. Usually, it's young bulls from other families that cause this kind of trouble. Often a bull of this age from within the family will be tolerated more so than an interloper looking for company.

Over time, adult females lose patience with young males. The females' message sinks in sooner or later, depending on the social situation of both the bull and the family. The bulls then go off on their own in search of new friends. This female was so fed up with this bull that he didn't even have time to swallow his drink before she forcefully sent him away, leaving him to drop his drink in retreat.

A lone young bull, Congo Connor, drinks under the starlit sky. He hasn't yet settled in with a stable group of males and is often found alone between male visits.

Lone young bulls at this age are most vulnerable to predation. Here, Bobtail's subadult sons test their strength by taunting this bull, but fortunately, they are not skilled enough to take him on for real.

Young bulls are also vulnerable to stirring up trouble with other, more dangerous animals, such as this black rhino. Since rhinos don't easily back down, and elephants are used to their paths being cleared merely by their approach, hackles are raised when a rhino doesn't give an elephant the right of way.

This young bull, Congo Connor (right), forges ties by leaning in to Tim (center) and then giving Willie Nelson a trunk-to-mouth greeting (facing page).

It takes time for a young bull to find his footing in the bull world. This young bull approaches an older bull in greeting, possibly to see if the older bull will tolerate a young apprentice. Although many older bulls take younger bulls under their wing, some have no interest in their company.

CHAPTER 5

The Boys' Club

In the arid environment of Etosha National Park, there are regions where groups of bulls appear to be larger and more tightly bonded than bull groups studied in less arid environments, particularly in dry years. Bull groups in our dry study area have strictly defined hierarchies in drier years. A strict hierarchy may help to reduce conflicts over limited resources when water and vegetation are scarce, and may determine who gets access to the best drinking water.

THE DON

The dominant bull of one of the bonded groups (aka "the boys' club") that we have been following over the last several years is named Greg (aka "the don").

I have been studying Greg since 2004. His character has been remarkably instructive of what it takes to be on top of the hierarchy and stay there through the best and worst of times, balancing aggression with the equivalent of back-slapping and morale-building among his constituency. The dry years are much easier than the wet years, as pecking orders are much more important to maintain when resources such as drinking water are low. Greg's position is more tenuous in wet years, as the younger bulls explore larger territories and tend to take more chances with their elders, and more musth bulls frequent the area in search of females in estrus.

For years now, whenever Greg strides up to the waterhole, the other bulls in the boys' club slowly back away, allowing him access to the best water. And when Greg settles in to drink, each bull in turn approaches him with an outstretched trunk, dipping the tip into Greg's mouth as though kissing a real don's ring. After performing the ritual, each bull's shoulders seem to relax at seeing their don placated, and each moves down to a lower-ranking position, away from Greg's preferred water, in the elephantine equivalent of a male social club.

This ritual greeting of the don is a recurring event that never fails to impress me—one of those reminders in life that human beings are not as unique in our social complexity as we sometimes like to think. The society of elephants is also profoundly steeped in ritual.

Dominance among bulls appears to be maintained through a delicate balance between friendly and aggressive behavior. While higher-ranking bulls exhibit more aggressive behavior than subordinate bulls, they also extend a surprising number of friendly gestures.

We also discovered that some bulls usually seem to prefer the company of two or more other males—what I term "buddies"—revealing that male elephants are much more social than previously thought, and maybe more social in drier environments.

MALE BONDING

Sparring as a ritual is also an important aspect of male bonding with older bulls, as illustrated by Willie and Tim's meditative Tai Chi spar in the sequence of photos on pages 138–39. Such ritual is evident in many all-male human societies as well, from fraternity hazings to boot-camp initiations to religious ceremonies.

Ritualized dominance behaviors within these bonded male groups are thought to formalize status relationships, where acts of subordination toward dominant individuals may serve to preempt aggression and thus generate greater tolerance among group members—hence the ceremonial stoop and kiss of the mafia don's ring to quell any thought of insubordination, disloyalty, or coalition formation against the don.

MALE AGGRESSION

Aggression in male elephants is often very subtle, where a slight lifting of the head or a foot toss may disclose less than cordial relations between two individuals. But, every once in a while, aggression is exhibited in extremely violent outbursts, where a tusk wound could result in death.

Jack Nicholson and Luke Skywalker engage in an intimate trunk wrap. Such intimate physical engagement requires mutual trust as neither elephant is in the position to attack or defend itself.

Prince Charles (on the left) and Beckham hurl themselves at each other like two locomotives.

Frankie Fredericks, the don's henchman (on the left), clobbers the newcomer that seems to have offended Greg in some way.

While we are in the middle of setting up camp in June, 2007, Greg (center), the elephant don, comes to Mushara for a midday drink with part of his entourage, unperturbed by our hammering and clanging. Not wanting to miss the opportunity, I steal away for a moment to take a photo and document their presence.

Younger core members of Greg's boys'
club rush in for a drink. It is unusual to
see males of this age so flustered (this is
accentuated by the draining temporal glands
seen next to the eyes of the bulls on the left
and right), but without older males around,
these subadult bulls can lose their cool
unexpectedly.

We know this dominant bull (above) is Greg (aka "the don") because of the two square notches in the lower portion of his left ear, along with his scraggly tail hair. But there is something else about him, something visible from a long way off that reveals his character. This guy has the confidence of a general—the way he holds his head, as well as his casual swagger. He also doesn't hesitate to show his affection for the younger bulls, as he does in the photo on the facing page. Here, he leans his head against little Hardy Boy's rear in a moment of what looks like pure affection, judging from Hardy Boy's lack of fear in remaining in the don's presence. He is a recent young recruit to the boys' club and is distinguishable by the keyhole cutout in the middle of his right ear.

Keeping good relations with the don is important, no matter how old one is. Here, the older Brendan (left) approaches Greg tentatively and breaks the tension (notice how Greg's ears are forward and pinched in the photo above, indicating agitation) with a trunk-to-mouth greeting (facing page). We assume that Brendan is at least as old or older than Greg, based on his shoulder height and the broadness of his head.

The extent of the intimacy of physical contact that occurs between close male allies is often surprising to the uninitiated. Male elephants can be extremely social, particularly if there are younger bulls in the mix. On the left, the trunk-over-head gesture is often a gentle reminder of dominance, or an attempt to stake a claim of dominance, but usually ends in an amicable spar. On the facing page, both elephants are placing their trunks in each other's mouth. Males with close bonds spend much of their time at the waterhole in close contact, even if it's just their tails or backsides that are touching.

Willie (left) and Tim (right) engage in a gentle spar. Willie is more senior and higher ranking than Tim but these two elephants share a special bond and neither has ever shown aggression toward the other. They will often engage in a long and slow sparring session like this one that seems more like an extended greeting than a test of dominance.

A balance of aggression and friendly behavior helps to maintain bonds among bull elephants. But in this case, there is no place for a friendly hello. The mid-ranking bull named Frankie Fredericks (on the left), who seemed to act as a henchman for Greg (after the disappearance of Torn Trunk), attacks a newcomer whose presence is clearly agitating Greg from a distance. Dust flies as the two goliaths hurtle at each other, massive heads raised, ears folded—first a squeak of leather, then a crack of colliding ivory. The assailant is initially undeterred and keeps coming at Frankie, but Frankie doesn't miss a beat. He doles out the blows with greater purpose than I had previously witnessed in a bull standing his ground. He pushes his opponent all the way to the edge of the clearing, holding this new bull in a withering stare until the loser relents, heads out, and disappears into the tree line.

Relationships can be tricky and need constant maintenance, but it pays to have someone watching your back. There are some males, however, who just seem to prefer to be on their own.

Evidence of coalition behavior is sometimes hard to find. Often behaviors are so subtle, it's not clear that a group is ganging up on an individual for whatever reason. But there are times like the moment this photo was taken where there is no mistaking a coordinated effort to intimidate this arriving bull.

Marlon Brando defends Willie against Scar (from right to left).

Scar approaches from the left, while Willie and Marlon drink with one eye on the intruder. Scar confronts Willie (top right), and Willie anxiously curls the bottom of his trunk. Just as he is being displaced, Marlon steps in.

Marlon Brando quickly becomes quite the formidable defensive backup for Willie with his head held high (notice the slope of the back) and ears held out as he marches toward Scar to put him in his place. Just the threat of his posture is enough to cause Scar to back down and walk off, eyeing Marlon over his shoulder in case he were to change his mind and charge.

Chapter 6

Sex in Bull City

It was midnight at our little oasis when an extremely young female in estrus arrived precipitously from the south, and chaos broke loose. She had clearly been harassed by a group of young males for some time, and her family was in a state of confusion as seven young bulls trailed the group, their exuberance for her being the cause of the disturbance. The riotous group made it to the waterhole with an explosion of splashing, screaming, and trumpeting as everyone tried to drink and at the same time avoid trouble.

While watching this young female's seemingly desperate retreat, I finally understood why, as studies have shown, females might prefer mating with an older musth bull over a young male. Apparently, the average female elephant is smart enough to choose a mate who will overcome all the competition, leaving her in peace with only a single bull. However, such was not the case in the scenario we witnessed. Without a musth bull, our young estrous female could be in for many hours of running with seven or more young bulls in hot pursuit.

Our research team enjoyed the fact that whenever a mating event took place, jubilant postcopulatory rumbles filled the night air. Quite often we heard monotone calls of unusually long duration (sometimes lasting forty seconds or so) that consisted of a series of overlapping rumbles, seemingly from many of the family group members. If elephants wanted to get the word out that a mating event had just happened, this was surely a resounding proclamation. But there were no such rumbles on this night. In the chaos, the young female ran off into the night with a storm of males in hot pursuit.

Musth Demystified

Mature male elephants normally enter the hormonal state of musth in their mid- to late twenties. Musth was first described in the Indian elephant, the Persian origin meaning "drunk." This heightened sexual state manifests itself in a suite of exaggerated and aggressive displays that other bulls seem to understand quite well, as they tend to give the musth bull the right of way.

Individuals in musth are thought to rise to the top of the dominance hierarchy, and thus get first crack at a female in estrus. Over the years of our research, we have found some exceptions to this rule, but in general it is thought that estrous females prefer to mate with musth bulls. An elephant in musth is looking for a mate with such singularity of purpose that he hardly takes the time to eat or drink. This explains why male elephants need to be in very good condition in order to be able to enter into and maintain musth. Musth bulls that get injured fall out of musth very quickly.

Bulls in the general elephant population enter musth one by one, rather than all at once, as antelope do when in rut. Dominant individuals tend to go into musth when more females are in estrus. But dominant bulls don't have all the advantages. Females in estrus have a say in the mating game and appear to pick favorites. To add to this dynamic, there is a certain percentage of mating that occurs with bulls that are not in musth, indicating that the state of musth does not always guarantee mating success.

When I show an audience a photograph of a male elephant at the height of musth—prancing and waving his trunk in front of his face—I often ask whether they think the bull in the image looks friendly or aggressive. More often than not, the answer is "friendly."

As you know by now, this couldn't be further from the truth. And if you weren't certain, just watch the response of any non-musth bull to this behavior, and the meaning of the gestures will become abundantly clear.

Beckham is a very interesting musth bull who showed up in 2008 and has entertained us ever since. He got his name because of his excessive foot-tossing behavior toward other bulls, reminding us of the famous soccer player David Beckham.

Beckham is of the prime age to easily dispense with challengers when in musth, yet he doesn't display aggression as much as we would have expected. In the 2010 season, there were several other formidable bulls in musth aside from Beckham, including Marlon Brando and Prince Charles. Since Marlon Brando appears to be about five years older than Beckham (judging by his height and the width of his skull), we thought for sure there would be a clash of the titans. But this was far from the case. Marlon Brando and Beckham had a remarkably amicable encounter with a mutual trunk-to-mouth greeting and no sign of aggression.

Just when we were ready to throw out every preconception we had about musth, in marched Prince Charles. Beckham showed no tolerance for this brutish contemporary and immediately clobbered his musthy challenger. The photo sequence on pages 162–65 illustrates the intense interaction, from which Prince Charles ultimately backed down and retreated, with Beckham escorting him out of the clearing.

Bulls in musth often travel great distances alone in search of females in estrus.

Smokey (left) is our most dramatic musth bull. You can see him coming from a long way off, dramatically curling his trunk across his face and dusting himself.

Females in estrus have a say in the mating game and appear to pick their favorites, usually an older bull in musth. Because gestation is about 22 months and lactation another two years, there can be three to nine years between ovulation periods that only last a few days. This means a very narrow window for reproduction. So, when a female is in estrus, there are often many attending bulls that follow the family. Mate guarding by musth bulls can minimize the amount that a female is hassled by other interested suitors, but it doesn't rule out the opportunistic interloper that may also find the opportunity to mate with the estrus female.

Musth bulls are often seen curling their trunks across their brows and waving their ears—presumably to facilitate the wafting of a sticky, musthy secretion from temporal glands located above their cheeks and just behind their ears. They do this while dribbling urine or leaking it in a wide stream. Testosterone levels can double or triple that of normal levels during this period. At this time, bulls are particularly interested in the hormonal status of females. On the facing page, a bull tests the estrus status of a female by smelling her urine and then placing his trunk up into the roof of his mouth (where the vomeronasal organ resides). He then curls his lip, exhibiting something called the flehmen response, an action which draws scents up into the vomeronasal organ.

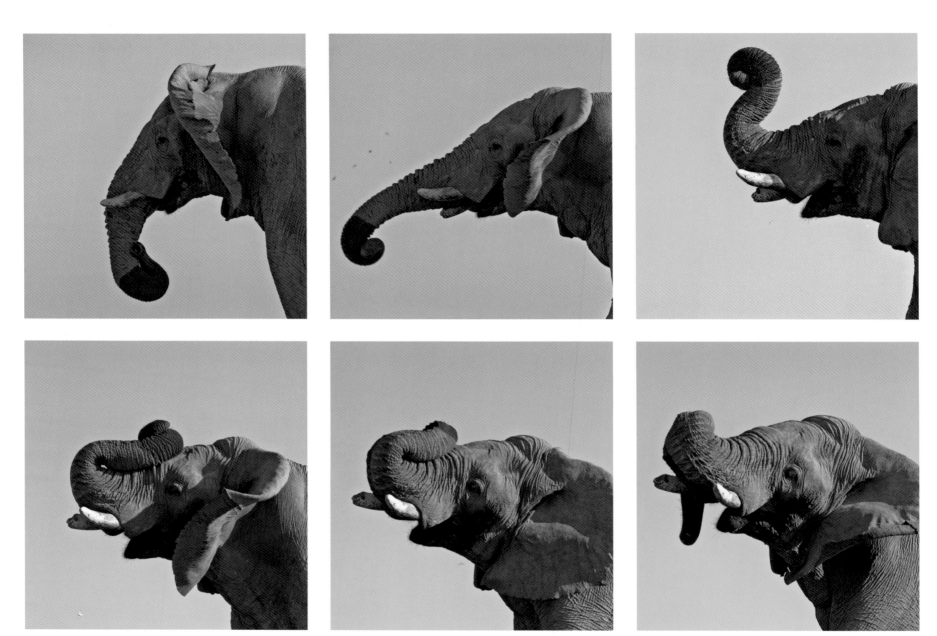

The ritualized trunk curl exhibited by a bull in musth alerts other bulls of his hormonal status. The behavior also has the practical purpose of spreading the sticky musth secretion from the temporal gland in the cheek area from one side of the face to the other. The musth bull engages in this activity while waving each ear individually. The waving of the ears serves to waft the heavy scent, which is thought to deter males and attract females (like a pheromone). In this photo sequence, Smokey performs the ritual while incorporating dust to add to the drama.

Here, Smokey waves his ears and trunk as if they are on fire and he can't put them out. He even prances as if his feet are burning. He is definitely more riled up than usual, kicking up dust as he makes his way across the plain, but there isn't another bull in sight. So what's his target? It's clear that his musth threat is effective on other species, as a giraffe quickly gets out of his way. When Smokey passes the giraffe and heads straight for our vehicle, we too make a hasty retreat as musth bulls are unpredictable and could charge us.

This photo sequence illustrates the intense interaction between musthy Prince Charles (left) and our boy Beckham (right). Clearly, Beckham had no tolerance for his opponent, and Prince Charles ultimately backed down and retreated.

Since Prince Charles (left) and Beckham (right) are both formidable bulls, and both happen to be in musth at the same time, we expected a real clash of the titans when they showed up at the waterhole. But after an intense few moments of heavy sparring, the contest seemed to be settled, with Prince Charles backing off, trunk outstretched toward the winner (this page, bottom photo). In such battles, it is vital to stay square with one's opponent, negotiating stabbing tusks with one's trunk. This explains all of the white tusk marks on Beckham's trunk that are his accumulation of battle scars during the season.

During some down time, we entertained ourselves with crazy, musthy Beckham, who had become a frequent visitor to our camp One day, after rolling around on the ground, sitting on the bunker (facing page), and tossing his trunk over his head, he tried to break the water pump, since a leak had made a fresh water pool underneath and he appeared to want more than a trickle. Next, he came over to investigate camp, as ramped up as we had seen any bull in musth.

Beckham (left) also uses the bunker as a negotiating table with rival, Kevin (right). The interaction ends more cordially than expected given both of their feisty temperaments and Beckham's hormonal status. Perhaps Kevin knew he should be on his best behavior.

(Facing page) In an effort to access fresh water directly from the spring, Beckham inspects our leaky water pump that we had very recently fixed. With the force he is using during his inspection, it appears that he intends to remove the whole barrel containing the pump. Fortunately, he stopped pushing before actually breaking the pump. Elephants are known to break water installations on farms in dry areas outside the park to access fresh water, so this may not have been the first time that Beckham has attempted such a feat. Next to the pump, Beckham and other elephants dug a shallow area and removed the rocks around the pump near the leak in order to form a pool of fresh water from which to drink.

I had always somehow felt that if elephants were not allowed to investigate their turf, they'd take their revenge at a later time. Perhaps this was a misguided sentiment, but I didn't want to turn the electric fence on Beckham until it got dark. Sure enough, Beckham walked right up to the fence and brought the two fingers of his trunk tip within centimeters of the fence. This behavior told me that he was keenly aware of what an electric fence was all about. He spent a few minutes inspecting the fence in this manner before circling the camp and coming around to size up the vehicles. Sometimes one loses perspective of just how large an elephant bull really is until the bull is standing next to something for scale. He could have crushed the cars in a heartbeat, and by his hesitation, I couldn't help but wonder whether he was contemplating doing just that.

CHAPTER 7

The End of a Reign

A WOUNDED DON

In the middle of the 2010 field season, Greg, the don of the boys' club, finally returned to Mushara after several weeks of absence. He was alone. And he was grumpy. It didn't take long for us to realize why. He was also wounded. He had a hole in the bottom of his trunk, probably due to an abscess from a wound. It took two or three times the normal amount of water for Greg to get enough to drink, as most of it spilled out of one nostril. An elephant's trunk is an extension of its nose, and as such, there are two chambers within the trunk, just like our two nasal passages. An elephant sucks water up into its trunk by breathing in and then exhales water into its mouth.

Greg's trunk wound has resulted in a large hole in the bottom section of his right nasal passage such that water pours right out of the hole as soon as Greg sucks water up. By the time he lifts his trunk to his mouth, half of the water has drained out, making it much more difficult for him to drink the amount of water he needs to survive.

We have already seen the effects of this wound on his health, as he is much thinner now than he has been in previous years. And the wound has also taken a toll on his social life, as he shuns the company of his contemporaries but does allow his younger contingent to accompany him on occasion.

As we were packing up to leave for the season, Greg came in for one of his long drinking sessions with some of his new young recruits. The younger bulls had long since left by the time Greg finished soaking his trunk and was ready to depart. He initiated his usual rumbling bout as he left, despite being alone. He rumbled and rumbled—his long, low calls unanswered—as if engaging in an old habit that wouldn't die. It was a haunting scene.

I stopped and watched through my night vision scope. I couldn't help but feel sorry for him as he stood at the edge of the clearing. Was he waiting for a buddy?

Later, as I was finishing up my packing, I heard two bulls rumbling in the distance. I looked through my night vision scope again and saw that Greg was now with Keith. Perhaps the don was indeed waiting for his entourage to show up, and Keith, having already been in for a drink hours earlier, had returned to collect him. Greg and Keith walked out together, each in turn rumbling while flapping his ears. They lumbered up a path and out of sight, just like in the good old days.

Perhaps the don's rallying wasn't merely an old habit. Perhaps he will pull through this difficult time and remain on top of the boys' club after all. But I know it isn't likely. With this wound, Greg's position as don of the boys' club will be challenged sooner than we had hoped. Old age would otherwise have been the likely cause for him to step down, as he would eventually lack the fitness to successfully challenge contenders.

Although Greg's dominance has waxed and waned depending on resource availability, he always came out on top of the hierarchy when it was indeed in place. In dry years, the linear hierarchy within the boys' club was evident in Greg's influence on the others. He has enjoyed this influence even over associates who were in musth.

But in years of high rainfall, like 2006, his influence came into question, particularly with musth bulls outside the boys' club, such as Smokey. And yet, in 2007 he was back on top of the hierarchy with a long line of associates following in his wake. In 2008 and 2009, higher rainfall meant smaller groups of associates, as there were more places to drink and the boys' club movements spread out over a wider range. Within these smaller groups, Greg was still on top, but there was more aggression evident between him and some of the other higher-ranking bulls. The hierarchy was not so clear-cut and linear. The other bulls, such as Abe, Marlon Brando, and Kevin, may well be the contenders for future don.

The would-be king will most likely step down to one of the other high-ranking bulls, as he will no longer be able to challenge them. Given that his wound is unlikely to heal, I predict an amicable deposition without contest, since he avoided high-ranking bulls in 2010. And when Greg's reign of dominance ends, the question will remain whether he will choose to take a backseat within the boys' club and accept the new dominant bull as his don, or become more of an outsider, visiting lower-ranking associates at the waterhole from time to time. Or will he become a loner, like some of the other elderly bulls within the population? It will be interesting to see how he is treated by the new dominant male.

There are several elderly bulls that Greg will not tolerate for some reason—probably as a result of something that happened long ago. Will this same kind of grudge be exhibited between Greg and the new don as Greg ages? It's hard to say, but it's clear that Greg has had enough history with many of the area's more dominant younger bulls that a few might relish the opportunity to keep the elderly Greg at a distance.

Although we have no real way to measure an elephant's sense of loss, many have witnessed elephants visiting their dead friends and relatives long after an elephant's passing, exploring the body with their feet, trunks, and tusks. Elephants seem very curious about death and will even visit the bones of others who would not be recognizable, but are perhaps in some way remembered. When Greg passes, no doubt his closest associates will know that he is no longer with them. And perhaps they will miss him and the heyday of his reign over the boys' club.

It takes Greg two to three times longer to drink because of his injured trunk.

Greg spends much time soaking his trunk wound in the pan, so much so that his younger companions have a hard time waiting for him to complete his soaking regime. He is now much thinner, his spine more exposed and his ribs visible, and his grouchy demeanor most likely speaks to his discomfort.

In 2005, at the height of his reign, Greg approaches the waterhole to drink (left in top photo on this page), and two other top-ranking bulls (Mike and Kevin) move off to the right (on the far side of the trough near the bunker) well before Greg arrives at the head of the trough. It's clear from this sequence of photos that a subadult male lion sitting on the bunker poses little threat to adult male elephants while they drink.

Facing page: In this sequence recorded in the very wet year of 2006, Greg approaches the water with Torn Trunk and Johannes and is confronted by the musthy Smokey (on right). Greg immediately veers away from Smokey (bottom photo), our first experience of Greg backing down to another bull. Although Greg had been able to defeat high-ranking musth bulls within his own club, Smokey posed an entirely different challenge that apparently Greg was not willing to contend with. In as much as Greg is the don of his local club, Smokey may turn out to be the *capo di tutti capi* of the Namutoni region. But we've never seen Smokey outside of his musth period, so things could look quite different for him socially in another season.

In another confrontation, Greg practically leaped out of his skin, ears folded in outrage that the old Captain Pickard would dare to approach the water after he and Torn Trunk made it quite clear with their body language that he was not welcome. They confronted the captain on the way to the waterhole, standing shoulder to shoulder, holding their heads and ears out in warning. But the captain was thirsty and continued on to the water, only to face even more aggression.

Despite losing his entourage, Greg still had loyal underlings that sought him out and paid their respects to the don, as if nothing had changed.

Tim tests the electric fence to make sure that it is working properly with enough of a deterring shock to keep curious critters at bay.

CHAPTER 8

Camp Life

Camp life at Mushara has its many perks as well as some challenges. Our five-star "Mushara cafe" (rating given by team members over the years) offers butternut squash cooked more ways than you probably thought possible, all of these recipes being camp favorites. Why butternut squash? Because it lasts. The camp has two solar refrigerators the size of a carry-on bag, so food preservation is a challenge, particularly since I buy most of our five-week supply in Windhoek before the season starts. One must be very creative in the kitchen to keep things interesting. There's also the small matter of staying clean despite stringent restrictions on water usage. But the elephants, the lions, and all the other animals make it all worth it—as well as the night sky, of course.

.When the elephants are not around, we're either taking photographs of other animals, preparing a meal, or indulging in the rare luxury of hair-washing.

I've spent many of my birthdays at Mushara, and whenever possible, I try to bring enough fresh eggs to make chocolate mousse from scratch for the camp to celebrate the big day.

It's always hard to pack up at the end of the season, but when we do, only the tower remains as well as all of our memories.

AFTERWORD

Almost twenty years ago, when I first started out at Mushara, I conducted most of my research in the bunker sixty feet away from the waterhole. Back then it was just me, my hammock, my tape recorder, microphone, and a small gas cooker to heat up tea and soup. As I listened to the bull elephants drinking, I would look out at the Southern Cross and wonder where my life might lead. Life has since become much more comfortable in the three-story tower where I now conduct my research, but sometimes I do miss the simplicity of those days, the meditative time, the elephants' slow, contemplative breathing and their unhurried, ponderous drinking. It was not only a simpler time for me, but also for the elephants.

With the human population increasing in some areas around the park, interactions between elephants and people are on the rise, and with more interaction tends to come more conflict. In areas just north of the park boundary, there has been an increase in human habitation, and elephants that have traditionally left the park in the wet season are coming into conflict with humans. I'm hoping that our research into male elephant society will provide important information to conservationists who are called upon to anticipate problems and facilitate better outcomes for the elephants.

It is my hope that our research on male elephant bonds will serve as a reminder (only for those that might need one) that many old bulls are not just lone, wandering souls out there. They are part of a larger, complex social network in which there are youngsters that depend on their elders for guidance, protection, and companionship at different stages of their lives.

Meanwhile, the soap opera of the boys' club will carry on whether or not I am there to witness its members in a rapidly changing landscape, to document the shifting of the social tide from year to year. I just hope that I'm able to be a part of it somehow, to continue my vigil for as long as I can find a way to support it and for as long as I'm welcome back.

Tyler came to visit me in the bunker at the end of the 2009 season. It was hard to believe it was him, seeing how much larger he appeared at this close proximity than he did from the tower and next to his older buddies, but sure enough, the small hole in the middle of his right ear gave him away. He was definitely coming into his own in the boys' club, and I looked forward to watching him continue to grow and mature within his extended social network.

PHOTOGRAPHER'S NOTE

Wildlife photography has its inherent difficulties—whether it's in trying to capture a rare moment on the fly, such as a predator catching its prey in its jaws, or a fleeting moment of aggression between two bull elephants. Obviously, having a camera with a fast autofocus lens is key. Then there are the issues of distance from your subject and shutter speed. These are challenges that any photographer shooting a moving target will face, whether it's the sports photographer or the wildlife photographer.

The advent of digital photography has revolutionized the playing field of photography for all photographers. We no longer have to guess (and hope) that our shot was a success and wait until the roll of film is processed. In the early days of our fieldwork, my husband Tim and I had to wait six to nine months to develop our film. With digital photography, we no longer have to worry about film expiration dates or whether our rolls of film were exposed to too many airport X-ray machines (needless to say, this was often a concern when traveling to and from Africa every year).

Tim and I now shoot with a Nikon D700, a full-frame digital camera with an ISO of 6400 and many, many features that we are still learning how to master. Our favorite and most versatile lens is the Nikon 80–200mm zoom lens with an f-stop of 2.8. And in the past few years, there have been a few very good teleconverters on the market. This has added to our flexibility and range without the added weight, size, and cost of more powerful low-light zoom lenses, such as the equivalent 400mm or 500mm lenses.

Digital photography allows remarkable flexibility and power. For example, under harsh daytime conditions in the desert, shooting on manual and adjusting your shutter speed and f-stop settings, guided by your histogram display, can help you capture an image with richer colors and more saturation than if you were to keep your camera locked on aperture or shutter speed mode (keeping your f-stop constant and varying your shutter speed, or vice-versa).

Trusting your histogram will go a long way to making sure that you captured everything in your images (even though they will look blown out on your camera monitor) without the instinct to underexpose to compensate for the harsh lighting. When you go to work with your images in Adobe Lightroom or any other image processing software, the shadows in an underexposed image will actually be too dark, and there is nothing you can do to bring information back from the black portions of your image. Hence, overexposure under harsh lighting conditions always gives you better results. This is where you have to learn not to assess image quality, with regard to lighting, using your camera monitor. It's like flying a plane at night. Trust your instruments and you will prevail!

The biggest challenge to photographing elephants, which is not something you necessarily think about until you are faced with the challenge, is depth of field and lighting conditions. Since elephants are so large, it is sometimes difficult to get the whole animal in focus during a shot. Fortunately, catching an elephant in action is a lot different from catching a hummingbird in action, and you can afford to sacrifice some shutter speed for depth of field.

The faster the shutter speed, the shallower the depth of field, which may mean that you have the elephant's trunk in focus right in front of you, but its body and perhaps its offspring will be out of focus. If you have enough light to afford slowing down the shot, you'll get more of the elephant in focus by creating a larger depth of field. You have to learn how to balance these two variables in order to perfect a shot. Granted, this problem only

presents itself if you are lucky enough to be very close to your elephantine subject, which we are when we're in our observation bunker at Mushara.

The other challenge, as I mentioned, is lighting. The most modern digital cameras have very high ISO values in the range of 6400. This allows you a tremendous amount of flexibility at sunset when elephant family groups tend to show up at the waterhole to drink. A higher ISO setting allows you to let more light into your camera sensor, thus letting you take a faster shot under lower light conditions than you otherwise could. But there is always a trade-off. While a higher ISO setting gives you more light, it also introduces more noise, and thus more grain, into the digital image. It is important to make a wise judgment call on what you are sacrificing and whether the sacrifice of the extra grain is necessary or worth it.

There comes a point in time when you just have to turn off the camera for the night, unless of course you are interested in getting a time lapse of a lone elephant bull under the Milky Way, or even a longer time lapse of the Southern Cross moving across the sky. Here's where a tripod is essential, as well as the highest ISO setting your camera offers.

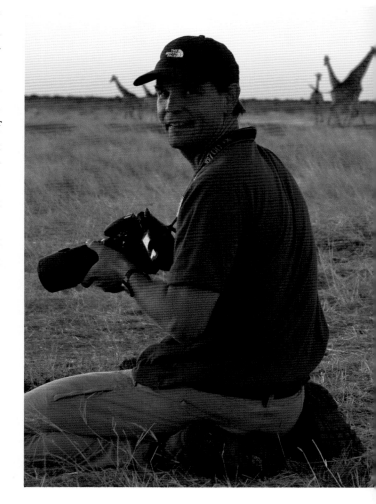

With these few insights into elephant photography, we hope you enjoy your next elephant photographic safari!

You never knows when a photographic moment will present itself. Here, this baby gave me a little solo photo shoot with his mom waiting in the wings behind him. This moment was fleeting, however, as she quickly moved forward and stood next to her baby; she loomed above me while I stood precariously on the edge of the ladder within the bunker in order to continue snapping away before she gave me a head shake, forcing me to retreat to safety within the hatch. My field assistant, Yoshi Hirano, took this shot of me from the tower.

ACKNOWLEDGMENTS

I always hate saying goodbye to Mushara, to Greg and his boys' club, and to Big Momma and her family. I'd like to thank them for sharing their home and their experience with us, and for their patience with our presence throughout the years.

Tim and I would like to thank the Namibian government for allowing us to conduct our research at Mushara waterhole for so many years. It has been a great privilege and we have many people to thank. We thank the folks at Etosha Ecological Institute, particularly Wilferd Versveld, Werner Kilian, and Johannes Kapner, for all of their help and support. We'd also like to thank Rehabeam Erckie and Immanuel Kapofi for all of their support from the Namutoni Ranger Station, and Windhoek staff, Malan and Pauline Lindeque and Ben Beital for their support of our research over the years, as well as Jo Tagg for his logistical support and enthusiasm.

We thank the core members of our research field team that worked with us during the time in which the majority of these photos were taken, particularly Colleen Kinzley, the general curator of the Oakland Zoo; all of the exceptional Stanford students that participated in and contributed to this research; and Stanford colleagues, Donna Bouley, Robert Sapolsky, Simon Klemperer, and Sunil Puria who contributed to this research.

Thanks also to Jason Wood, from the Department of Psychology at the University of Washington, who has been working with me on data analysis through the years, and Sam Wasser and his lab for the hormone analysis. A big thank-you to my agent, Ann Downer-Hazell, at Elefolio for helping me develop this book from conception to its final form. Also a big thank you to the folks at GPP, particularly Melissa Evarts, layout artist, and Greg Hyman, project editor, as well as my editor Holly Rubino who cared deeply about this project and who have all worked extremely hard to make this book as beautiful as it is. Thanks also to Utopia Scientific (www.utopiascientific.org) and our contributing volunteers that participated in this research, Stanford University faculty and VPUE student summer grants, and several small grants from the U.S. Fish and Wildlife Service and the National Geographic Society. Lastly, we'd like to thank Paul Kennedy and Sue McConnell for their generous advice on photography under extremely challenging conditions.

Do you want to help make a difference for elephants? Depending on the field season, we often accept a few contributing volunteers as Utopia Scientific research assistants to help collect data for our ongoing elephant research. By lending your expertise (or even just your enthusiasm and an extra pair of eyes), your participation helps support the running of the project. If you'd prefer the armchair approach to support, you can also sponsor a specific elephant or make a contribution to the Mushara Elephant Project. Please visit the website for Utopia Scientific (www.utopiascientific.org) and contact us if you are interested in participating in any of these programs.

ABOUT THE AUTHOR AND PHOTOGRAPHERS

Dr. Caitlin O'Connell is a faculty member in the Department of Otolaryngology, Head & Neck Surgery at Stanford University School of Medicine, and a world-renowned expert on elephants. She has dedicated the past twenty years of her research to understanding how elephants communicate and how their societies are constructed and maintained, resulting in numerous scientific publications. She is now applying what she has learned about vibrotactile sensitivity in elephants to helping people with hearing impairments.

She is the author of the internationally acclaimed science memoir *The Elephant's Secret Sense* and has coauthored the children's book *The Elephant Scientist*. Her essays have appeared in a number of popular magazines, including *Smithsonian* and *Africa Geographic*.

All of her books and essays feature her photography as well as that of her husband, Timothy Rodwell, MD, PhD, MPH, an assistant professor at the University of California, San Diego in the department of Medicine.

Together they have developed a photo and video library of all aspects of elephant life over the twenty-year course of their research in Etosha National Park, Namibia. These photos have appeared in numerous national and international popular, wildlife, and science magazines, including *National Geographic*, *Smithsonian* magazine, and *Africa Geographic*.

O'Connell and Rodwell cofounded the nonprofit organization Utopia Scientific (www.utopiascientific.org), dedicated to research, conservation, and science education. They also founded and co-direct the production company Triple Helix Productions, which focuses on developing popular media products without sacrificing accurate scientific content. They have coauthored several screenplays and novels for young adults that incorporate basic science concepts. O'Connell teaches Science Writing for Stanford University and the New York Times Knowledge Network.

Visit the author at www.caitlinoconnell.com.

MAX SALOMON